For Peter Ives, Andrea Ayvazian, and Karen Hurd,
who worked so hard for so long to help bring the
statue of Sojourner Truth to Florence, Massachusetts
—A.T.

For Pops
—J.R.

Special thanks to Nell Irvin Painter and
Margaret Washington for their careful fact-checking.

My Name Is Truth
Text copyright © 2015 by Ann Turner
Illustrations copyright © 2015 by James Ransome

ISBN 978-0-06-075898-1 (trade bdg.) — ISBN 978-0-06-075899-8 (lib. bdg)

The artist used watercolors to create the illustrations for this book.
Typography by Megan Stitt
14 15 16 17 18 SCP 10 9 8 7 6 5 4 3 2 1
❖
First Edition

My Name Is TRUTH
The Life of Sojourner Truth

by Ann Turner   illustrated by James Ransome

HARPER
An Imprint of HarperCollinsPublishers

My mama was a slave woman called Mau-Mau
with sweet arms and eyes like a hawk
I had a daddy, too, Bomefree,

they loved all twelve of us
and had to see us sold off one by one
like horses for work

their hearts most broke.

Mama told me to look up at the stars an

...ight shining over my brothers and sisters

we never hardly saw them again

her heart had twelve holes in it
I know.

I got bought for $100 when I was nine
at least they spoke my tongue, *Dutch*—

next place (I was bigger now, worth $150)
they did not speak words I knew

I was always getting beat.

Once he fired up a bunch of green
sticks in the fire hardened like stone
and beat me until the blood ran

those marks will never go away
I can feel them like ridges under my dress.

Then Master Dumont bought me
he was not so bad
but the mistress was evil

they thought my back was a cart
for hauling rocks wood timber and grain

I worked hard as a man

did they ever see me,
Isabella, under those loads?

Time came he said,
"Isabella, you are a good woman,
you can go free one year early,"

but he broke his promise—

I determined to leave

I owned myself now
I was not a slave.

I spun 100 pounds of wool to make up for leaving, crept out of the door in the darkness,

my baby Sophia clutched in my arms and *ra*

would he chase me . . . would he *not* . . . until God showed me th

nd *walked* and *ran* and *walked* for miles looking over my shoulder . . .

y to a kind family that took me in, the baby too.

"Welcome," they said

had anyone ever said that word
to me before?

and showed me a fine wide room
with a white bed to sleep in,

I never slept in a bed before

just let me creep under and

t will be like a shelter of leaves,

finally sleep came to my eyes.

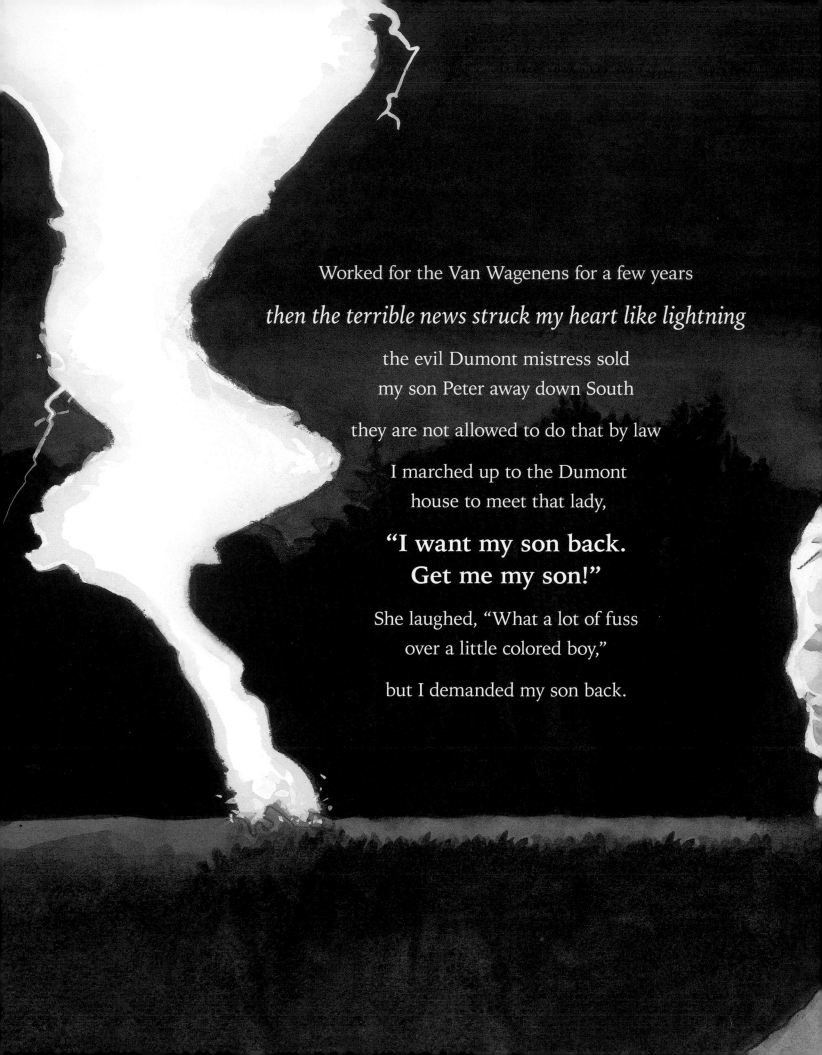

Worked for the Van Wagenens for a few years

then the terrible news struck my heart like lightning

the evil Dumont mistress sold
my son Peter away down South

they are not allowed to do that by law

I marched up to the Dumont
house to meet that lady,

**"I want my son back.
Get me my son!"**

She laughed, "What a lot of fuss
over a little colored boy,"

but I demanded my son back.

I got lawyers to help
and finally Peter came home again,
his back a mess of scars, his soul too,
frightened of his mama at first

but he came to know me at last.

I worked in New York City for a while—won't spend
long on that—met some bad people some good ones

but God was leading me East to preach
I left at dawn

and God spoke in my heart

a new name that fits me like

new dress made just for me

now I am *Sojourner* because I travel far and long
to tell the news of God's *truth* in meetings and gatherings—
people like to hear me talk

I think with a name like *Sojourner Truth*
a body has some *respect* at last.

I found a new home in Massachusetts
at a silk mill where all men and women were *equal*.

I was happy there, bought a little house—my very first—and preached even more.

One night at a camp meeting
there was a bunch of rowdies kicking up a storm
I was afraid they'd come for me
the only colored woman in the crowd

I hid behind a trunk
then my heart spoke,

Sojourner, are you weak?
Isn't God with you right now?

I strode out and climbed onto a wagon back,
spoke and sang and preached to those rowdies
till they were calm.

Something about my voice is like
a blanket on a fretful baby

then at times
my voice is like Gabriel's trumpet,

firing people up,
telling them the good news of salvation
and the terrible days of slavery.

People just can't believe an ex–slave woman
can speak truth and power

once at a rally a man jumped up and shouted,
**"You must be a man—you are tall
as one, powerful as one."**

"You want me to show you I am a woman?"

I threatened to open my dress but
others made him back down in shame

I showed them my truth then.

I've told my story to Olive Gilbert
a kind woman at the mill in Northampton.

I see all those words
creeping across the page as she writes.
(I never could make sense
of writing or reading!)

I will go on the road again selling my
Narrative of Sojourner Truth
and the photographs of me—

those shadow pictures bring in money
to feed the real woman.

Sometimes I sit in amazement
in some fine living room remembering—
I was a slave
working in sweat, beaten, sleeping on hard floors
now I sleep in a real bed and rally others with fiery words

I think of my daddy my brothers and sisters
like twelve shining stars

I will see them and my own children
again someday

Mama will put her sweet arms around me
and I will be home at last.

Who could have predicted that a baby born to slave parents in New York State in 1797 would turn out to be a prophetic preacher who would bring men and women to tears when she spoke? Born in a Dutch-speaking household to Mau-Mau ("mama" in Dutch) and Bomefree (from "tree" in Dutch), Isabella was one of ten to twelve slave children, most of them sold to different owners by the time she was born.

As Isabella recounted her own story years later, Mau-Mau would light a pine torch in the damp cellar of the slave-owner's house and tell Isabella about her brothers and sisters, now gone. At other times, Mau-Mau pointed to the sky and said God lived there, and whenever Isabella was beaten or sad, she could pray to Him for help. Sojourner Truth, the name she chose for herself later, did so all of her long life.

Isabella was sold several times before being bought by the Dumont family, where she stayed for sixteen years. As she grew into a tall, powerful woman, she said of herself: *I have as much muscle as any man, and can do as much work as any man. I have plowed and reaped and husked and chopped and mowed, and can any man do more than that?*[1]

Her owner, Mr. Dumont, worked Isabella as hard as a draft horse. New York State was set to free its slaves in 1827, but Mr. Dumont promised Isabella he would release her a year earlier. But when she badly injured her right hand, her owner went back on his promise, saying she could not work as hard.

But Isabella did not let that stop her. She escaped with her baby, Sophia, to a couple she knew, the Van Wagenens, who were against slavery. She had to leave her three other children behind, for as an escaped slave it would have been impossible to care for all of them.

A year after her escape, Isabella learned her five-year-old son, Peter, had been sold South by the Dumonts, which was against state law. With great determination and the help of the Quakers, she used the court system to get her son back. This was almost unheard of for a former slave at the time. As Isabella said, *I know and do what is right better than many big men who read.*[2]

Many years later, after living and working in New York City, Isabella chose her own name, Sojourner Truth—for she would always travel and she would always tell the truth. Seeking a place to live, she came to the Northampton Association for Education and Industry, a cooperative antislavery community in Massachusetts where people lived together and worked in a silk mill. There she met the abolitionist William Lloyd Garrison, who encouraged Sojourner to bring her antislavery message to a wider audience. She also met Olive Gilbert, who wrote down her story in *The Narrative of Sojourner Truth,* since Sojourner